This Notebook Belongs To:

ALEXANDER HAMILTON

Made in the USA
Coppell, TX
01 December 2019

12142776R00066